*To Tony and Kati
who love to tell
and listen to
good clean jokes*

Fabulous & Funny CLEAN JOKES for Kids!

Bob Phillips

Steve Russo

HARVEST HOUSE PUBLISHERS

EUGENE, OREGON

Scripture quotations in this book are taken from the King James Version of the Bible.

Cover by Terry Dugan Design, Minneapolis, Minnesota

FABULOUS AND FUNNY CLEAN JOKES FOR KIDS
Formerly titled *Wild & Wooly Clean Jokes for Kids*

Copyright © 1996 by Harvest House Publishers
Published by Harvest House Publishers
Eugene, Oregon 97402

ISBN 0-7369-1365-3

Printed in the United States of America

06 07 08 09 10 11 / BC-MS / 10 9 8 7 6 5 4

Contents

Barnaby & Basil

Barnaby: What candy do kids on the school playground like to eat?
Basil: I have no clue.
Barnaby: Recess pieces.

❖　❖　❖

Barnaby: What's green and red all over?
Basil: I don't know.
Barnaby: A cucumber with a sunburn.

❖　❖　❖

Barnaby: Why did the man with amnesia take up running?

Basil: I have no clue.
Barnaby: He wanted to jog his memory.

❖   ❖   ❖

Barnaby: What do you call a chicken running down the road?
Basil: I can't guess.
Barnaby: Fast food.

❖   ❖   ❖

Barnaby: What's green, black, and white?
Basil: I have no idea.
Barnaby: A car-sick zebra.

❖   ❖   ❖

Barnaby: What do you put on a pig when it hurts itself?
Basil: You tell me.
Barnaby: Oinkment.

❖   ❖   ❖

Barnaby: What animal goes to bed with it's shoes on?
Basil: I give up.
Barnaby: A horse.

❖ ❖ ❖

Barnaby: What is a mosquitoes favorite sport?
Basil: Who knows?
Barnaby: Skin diving.

❖ ❖ ❖

Barnaby: What kind of paper do mosquitoes like?
Basil: You've got me.
Barnaby: Scratch paper.

❖ ❖ ❖

Barnaby: What did one tonsil say to the other tonsil?
Basil: My mind is blank.
Barnaby: Hurry and get ready. The doctor is taking us out tonight.

❖ ❖ ❖

Barnaby: What did the thief say when he robbed the glue factory?
Basil: That's a mystery.
Barnaby: This is a stickup.

❖ ❖ ❖

Barnaby: What newspaper do cows read?
Basil: I'm blank.
Barnaby: *The Evening Moos.*

❖ ❖ ❖

Barnaby: What is full of ink and doesn't have any hair?
Basil: I don't have the foggiest.
Barnaby: A bald-point pen.

❖ ❖ ❖

Barnaby: What do you get when you cross a dalmatian and a pig?
Basil: It's unknown to me.
Barnaby: Spotted bacon.

❖ ❖ ❖

Barnaby: What did the penny say to the dime?
Basil: I'm in the dark.
Barnaby: Why don't I have more cents?

Barnaby: What did one computer say to the other at lunchtime?
Basil: Search me.
Barnaby: Let's grab a byte to eat!

❖ ❖ ❖

Barnaby: What do you call a cat that drinks lemonade?
Basil: You've got me guessing.
Barnaby: A sourpuss.

❖ ❖ ❖

Barnaby: What has 18 legs and catches flies?
Basil: How should I know?
Barnaby: A baseball team.

❖ ❖ ❖

Barnaby: What is purple and swings from a tree?
Basil: I don't know.
Barnaby: A gr-ape!

2

Lisa & Lola

Lisa: What do you get when you cross a monster and a new baseball player?
Lola: I have no clue.
Lisa: Rookie Monster.

❖ ❖ ❖

Lisa: What did the big flower say to the little flower?
Lola: I don't know.
Lisa: What's up, Bud?

❖ ❖ ❖

Lisa: What is a doctor's favorite musical instrument?

Lola: Beats me.
Lisa: An eardrum.

❖ ❖ ❖

Lisa: What kind of whale flies?
Lola: I can't guess.
Lisa: A pilot whale.

❖ ❖ ❖

Lisa: What do you call a train loaded with bubble gum?
Lola: I have no idea.
Lisa: A chew-chew train.

❖ ❖ ❖

Lisa: What kind of music does a mummy like best?
Basil: You tell me.
Lisa: Wrap music.

❖ ❖ ❖

Lisa: What do you drink at a football game?
Lola: I give up.
Lisa: Root beer.

❖ ❖ ❖

Lisa: What do you get when you cross a big white bear with a wig?
Lola: Who knows?
Lisa: Polar hair.

❖ ❖ ❖

Lisa: What are the smallest rooms in the world?
Lola: You've got me.
Lisa: Mushrooms.

❖ ❖ ❖

Lisa: What kind of ears do engines have?
Lola: That's a mystery.
Lisa: Engine-ears.

❖ ❖ ❖

Lisa: What is green and sings and dances?
Lola: I'm blank.
Lisa: Elvis Parsley.

❖ ❖ ❖

Lisa: What would two bedbugs do if they were in love?

Lola: I don't have the foggiest.
Lisa: They would get married in the spring.

❖   ❖   ❖

Lisa: What happens once in a minute, twice in a moment, but never in a thousand years?
Lola: It's unknown to me.
Lisa: The letter M.

❖   ❖   ❖

Lisa: What did one penny say to the other penny?
Lola: I'm in the dark.
Lisa: Let's get together and make some cents.

3

Bessie & Jessie

Bessie: Why would a heart be a good musical instrument?
Jessie: I have no clue.
Bessie: It has a great beat.

❖ ❖ ❖

Bessie: Why does Santa have a garden?
Jessie: I don't know.
Bessie: Because he likes to ho, ho, ho.

❖ ❖ ❖

Bessie: Why does a dog wag his tail?
Jessie: Beats me.

Bessie: Because no one else will wag it for him.

❖ ❖ ❖

Bessie: Why don't leopards play hide and seek?
Jessie: I can't guess.
Bessie: Because they're always spotted.

❖ ❖ ❖

Bessie: Why did the farmer name his pig Ink?
Jessie: I have no idea.
Bessie: Because it kept running out of the pen.

❖ ❖ ❖

Bessie: Why did the swimmer get a ticket?
Jessie: Beats me.
Bessie: He was caught diving without a license.

❖ ❖ ❖

Bessie: Why did the turtle cross the road?
Jessie: I give up.
Bessie: To get to the shell station.

❖ ❖ ❖

Bessie: Why did the turtle cross the road?
Jessie: Who knows?

Bessie: It was the chicken's day off.

❖ ❖ ❖

Bessie: Why is it so hard for a bank to keep a secret?
Jessie: You've got me.
Bessie: Because there are so many tellers.

❖ ❖ ❖

Bessie: Why did the old house go to the doctor?
Jessie: My mind is blank.
Bessie: It was having window panes.

❖ ❖ ❖

Bessie: Why is Alabama the smartest state?
Jessie: That's a mystery.
Bessie: Because it has four A's and a B.

❖ ❖ ❖

Bessie: Why are potato chips considered stupid?
Jessie: I'm blank.
Bessie: Because at parties they always hang around with the dips.

❖ ❖ ❖

Bessie: Why did the dragon breathe on a map of the earth?

Jessie: It's unknown to me.

Bessie: Because he wanted to set the world on fire.

❖ ❖ ❖

Bessie: Why do elephants paint their toenails red?

Jessie: I'm in the dark.

Bessie: To hide in the cherry trees.

❖ ❖ ❖

Bessie: Why did the punk rocker cross the street?

Jessie: I pass.

Bessie: He was stapled to the chicken.

❖ ❖ ❖

Bessie: Why did the poet go broke?

Jessie: You've got me guessing.

Bessie: Because rhyme doesn't pay.

4

Who's There?

Knock, knock.
Who's there?
Cow.
Cow who?
Cows say moo, not who!

❖ ❖ ❖

Knock, knock.
Who's there?
Happy.
Happy who?
Happy birthday to you!

❖ ❖ ❖

Knock, knock.
Who's there?
Soup.
Soup who?
Superman.

❖ ❖ ❖

Knock, knock.
Who's there?
Alex.
Alex who?
Alex plain later.

❖ ❖ ❖

Knock, knock.
Who's there?
Owl.
Owl who?
Owl never tell.

❖ ❖ ❖

Knock, knock.
Who's there?
Lettuce.
Lettuce who?
Lettuce in. It's cold outside.

❖ ❖ ❖

Knock, knock.
Who's there?
Dishes.
Dishes who?
Dishes me, open the door.

❖ ❖ ❖

Knock, knock.
Who's there?
Howl.
Howl who?
Howl I get in if you don't open the door?

❖ ❖ ❖

Knock, knock.
Who's there?
Mickey.
Mickey who?
Mickey is stuck in the lock.

5

Rufus & Maynard

Rufus: What do cows put on their ice cream?
Maynard: I have no clue.
Rufus: Chocolate moo-oo-se.

❖ ❖ ❖

Rufus: What is claustrophobia?
Maynard: I don't know.
Rufus: A huge fear of Santa Claus.

❖ ❖ ❖

Rufus: What do you get when you cross a chicken
and an earthquake?
Maynard: Beats me.

Rufus: Scrambled eggs.

❖ ❖ ❖

Rufus: What is a pig's favorite fairy tale?
Maynard: I can't guess.
Rufus: Slopping Beauty!

❖ ❖ ❖

Rufus: What makes a chicken laugh?
Maynard: I have no idea.
Rufus: A comedi-hen.

❖ ❖ ❖

Rufus: What did summer say to spring?
Maynard: You tell me.
Rufus: Help! I'm going to fall!

❖ ❖ ❖

Rufus: What do you get when you cross a centipede with a parrot?
Maynard: I give up.
Rufus: A walkie-talkie.

❖ ❖ ❖

Rufus: What food can never become the heavyweight champion of the world?
Maynard: Who knows?
Rufus: A lollipop. It always gets licked.

❖ ❖ ❖

Rufus: What should you do if you see a blue whale?
Maynard: You've got me.
Rufus: Try to cheer it up!

❖ ❖ ❖

Rufus: What fruit never goes anywhere alone?
Maynard: My mind is blank.
Rufus: Pears.

❖ ❖ ❖

Rufus: What is a duck's favorite ballet?
Maynard: That's a mystery.
Rufus: The Nutquacker.

❖ ❖ ❖

Rufus: What flowers does a person carry around with them all year long?
Maynard: I'm blank.
Rufus: Tulips (two lips).

❖ ❖ ❖

Rufus: What does a snake give his girlfriend on their first date?
Maynard: I don't have the foggiest.
Rufus: A good-night hiss.

❖ ❖ ❖

Rufus: What has an eye but cannot see?
Maynard: It's unknown to me.
Rufus: A sewing needle.

❖ ❖ ❖

Rufus: What do you call Jessie James when he has the flu?
Maynard: Search me.
Rufus: A sick shooter.

❖ ❖ ❖

Rufus: What kind of people go on diets?
Maynard: You've got me guessing.
Rufus: People who are thick and tired of their weight.

6

Stella & Agatha

Stella: What kind of car does a rich cat drive?
Agatha: I have no clue.
Stella: A Cat-illac.

❖ ❖ ❖

Stella: What do frogs like to eat with their hamburgers?
Agatha: I don't know.
Stella: French flies.

❖ ❖ ❖

Stella: What can't you have for breakfast?
Agatha: Beats me.
Stella: Lunch and dinner.

❖ ❖ ❖

Stella: What happened to the bee when he called his friend on the phone?
Agatha: I can't guess.
Stella: He got a bussssssy signal.

❖ ❖ ❖

Stella: What is the tallest building in the world?
Agatha: I have no idea.
Stella: A library because it has the most stories.

❖ ❖ ❖

Stella: What do chicks say when they're stuck in traffic?
Agatha: You tell me.
Stella: Peep peep!

❖ ❖ ❖

Stella: What did the sparrow say to his girl-friend?
Agatha: I give up.
Stella: You're real tweet.

❖ ❖ ❖

Stella: What did the chicken say when he was done eating?
Agatha: Who knows?
Stella: May I be egg-scused?

❖ ❖ ❖

Stella: What happens when a chicken eats too fast?
Agatha: You've got me.
Stella: It gets the chiccups.

❖ ❖ ❖

Stella: What kind of chicken can you buy for a penny?
Agatha: My mind is blank.
Stella: A chick that goes cheap.

❖ ❖ ❖

Stella: What is an owl's favorite food?
Agatha: That's a mystery.
Stella: Owl-ives.

❖ ❖ ❖

Stella: Why did Smokey the Bear retire?
Agatha: I can't guess.
Stella: He was burned out.

❖ ❖ ❖

Stella: What kind of jewelry do vegetables wear?
Agatha: I don't have the foggiest.
Stella: Onion rings.

❖ ❖ ❖

Stella: What bird wears a wig?
Agatha: I'm in the dark.
Stella: A bald eagle.

❖ ❖ ❖

Stella: What kind of tuba can't you play?
Agatha: Search me.
Stella: A tuba toothpaste.

❖ ❖ ❖

Stella: What is the difference between a famous ballerina and a duck?
Agatha: You've got me guessing.
Stella: One goes quick on her beautiful legs, and the other goes quack.

❖ ❖ ❖

Stella: What's sticky, purple, has 16 legs, and is
  covered with brown hair?
Agatha: I don't know?
Stella: I don't know either. But they're serving
  it for lunch today in the school cafeteria.

❖ ❖ ❖

Stella: What does a cow say when she wants to
  get away from the courthouse?
Agatha: How should I know?
Stella: She moos (moves) for a recess.

❖ ❖ ❖

Stella: Why did the pilot go to the psychologist?
Agatha: I pass.
Stella: He thought he was plane crazy.

7

Mork & Dork

Mork: Why did the boy who hated math want to take the math test?

Dork: I have no clue.

Mork: Because his teacher told him it would be a piece of cake!

❖ ❖ ❖

Mork: Why did the class clown give Jenny a dog biscuit?

Dork: I don't know.

Mork: He heard she was the teacher's pet.

❖ ❖ ❖

Mork: Why did the kid eat a dollar bill?
Dork: Beats me.
Mork: Because it was his lunch money.

❖ ❖ ❖

Mork: Why doesn't the corn like the farmer?
Dork: I can't guess.
Mork: Because he picks its ears.

❖ ❖ ❖

Mork: Why did the kids tell jokes in the mirror?
Dork: I have no idea.
Mork: To see it crack up.

❖ ❖ ❖

Mork: Why didn't the skeleton go to the dance?
Dork: You tell me.
Mork: He had no "body" to go with.

❖ ❖ ❖

Mork: Why shouldn't you tell a secret to a pig?
Dork: I give up.
Mork: Because it's a squealer.

❖ ❖ ❖

Mork: Why was the father catepillar so angry?
Dork: Who knows?
Mork: Because all of his children needed new shoes.

❖   ❖   ❖

Mork: Why are teachers like bank robbers?
Dork: You've got me.
Mork: They both want everybody to raise their hands.

❖   ❖   ❖

Mork: Why did the horse cross the road?
Dork: My mind is blank.
Mork: Because it was the chicken's day off.

❖   ❖   ❖

Mork: Why do cows have bells?
Dork: That's a mystery.
Mork: Because their horns don't work.

❖   ❖   ❖

Mork: Why did the bird go to the doctor?
Dork: I'm blank.
Mork: To get his tweetment.

❖ ❖ ❖

Mork: Why is the sky so high?
Dork: I don't have the foggiest.
Mork: So the birds won't bump their heads.

❖ ❖ ❖

Mork: Why did the turkey cross the road?
Dork: It's unknown to me.
Mork: Because he wasn't chicken.

❖ ❖ ❖

Mork: Why does the ocean roar?
Dork: I'm in the dark.
Mork: You would, too, if you had lobsters in your
  bed.

❖ ❖ ❖

Mork: Why wasn't the girl afraid of the shark?
Dork: Search me.
Mork: Because it was a man-eating shark.

❖ ❖ ❖

Mork: Why'd the man take two pairs of shorts
  to play golf?

Dork: You've got me guessing.
Mork: In case he got a hole in one.

❖ ❖ ❖

Mork: Why did the man put a radio in the refrigerator?
Dork: I pass.
Mork: To hear cool music.

❖ ❖ ❖

Mork: Why did the boy eat the encyclopedia?
Dork: How should I know?
Mork: Because he was hungry for knowledge.

❖ ❖ ❖

Mork: Why do you think I had to pay extra for the installation of this new rug?
Dork: I don't know?
Mork: Carpet tax (tacks).

8

Thelma & Anita

Thelma: Why did the woman run outside with her purse open?
Anita: I have no clue.
Thelma: She was expecting some change in the weather.

❖ ❖ ❖

Thelma: Why did the cookie go to the doctor?
Anita: I don't know.
Thelma: Because he felt crumb-y.

❖ ❖ ❖

Thelma: Why shouldn't you borrow a penny

from a football coach?

Anita: Beats me.

Thelma: Because he'll always want a quarter back.

❖ ❖ ❖

Thelma: Why didn't the skeleton cross the road?

Anita: I can't guess.

Thelma: Because he had no guts.

❖ ❖ ❖

Thelma: Why was the bull so stubborn?

Anita: I have no idea.

Thelma: Because he was bull-headed.

❖ ❖ ❖

Thelma: Why is a room full of couples considered empty?

Anita: You tell me.

Thelma: Because there's not a single person in it!

❖ ❖ ❖

Thelma: Why did the cherry run across the road?

Anita: I give up.
Thelma: Because she was berry scared of being eaten.

❖ ❖ ❖

Thelma: Why did the orange go to the hospital?
Anita: Who knows?
Thelma: Because it wasn't peeling well.

❖ ❖ ❖

Thelma: Why was 6 afraid of 7?
Anita: You've got me.
Thelma: Because 7, 8, 9.

❖ ❖ ❖

Thelma: Why didn't the skeleton use a towel after he took a shower?
Anita: My mind is blank.
Thelma: Because he was already bone dry.

❖ ❖ ❖

Thelma: Why do sea gulls live by the sea?
Anita: That's a mystery.
Thelma: Because if they lived by the bay, they would be bay gulls.

❖ ❖ ❖

Thelma: Why did the man put his dog in a
  bag?
Anita: I'm blank.
Thelma: It was a doggy bag.

❖ ❖ ❖

Thelma: Why are football stadiums so cold?
Anita: I don't have the foggiest.
Thelma: Because they have too many fans.

❖ ❖ ❖

Thelma: Why did Cinderella get thrown off the
  baseball team?
Anita: It's unknown to me.
Thelma: Because she ran away from the ball!

❖ ❖ ❖

Thelma: Why did the snowman refuse to get
  married?
Anita: How should I know?
Thelma: He got cold feet.

9

Grab Bag

A horse walks into a cafe and the waitress asks, "Why the long face?"

❖ ❖ ❖

This is a dirty joke: A man fell in the mud.

❖ ❖ ❖

Customer: Are you supposed to tip the waiter here?
Waiter: Yes!
Customer: Then tip me. I've been waiting an hour for my food!

❖ ❖ ❖

Teacher: Name six animals of the Arctic region.
Student: Three walruses and three polar bears.

❖ ❖ ❖

A man walked into a bar and asked for a cup of coffee without any cream. The waiter said, "Okay, just a minute" and went behind the bar. Three minutes later the waiter came back and said, "We are out of cream, how about a cup of coffee without any milk?"

❖ ❖ ❖

Q: In what kind of home does the buffalo roam?
A: A very dirty one.

❖ ❖ ❖

Q: A man rode into town on the fourth of July. He stayed a week and then left on the fourth of July. How is this possible?
A: The horse's name was 4th of July.

❖ ❖ ❖

Q: At what time do you go to the dentist?
A: "Tooth-hurty."

❖ ❖ ❖

Q: If a carrot and a cabbage ran a race, which one would win?
A: The cabbage, because it's a head.

❖ ❖ ❖

Q: If athletes get athlete's foot, what do astronauts get?
A: Missle toe.

❖ ❖ ❖

Q: Are baby skunks cute?
A: Yes, they're odorable.

❖ ❖ ❖

Q: Did you hear about the fire at the shoe factory?
A: 100 soles were lost. I bet some heel started it.

10

Reginald & Bartholomew

Reginald: Why did Tarzan lose the tennis match?
Bartholomew: I have no clue.
Reginald: Because he played against a cheetah.

❖ ❖ ❖

Reginald: Why is the man laughing up his sleeve?
Bartholomew: I don't know.
Reginald: Because that's where his funny bone is.

❖ ❖ ❖

Reginald: Why did the skeleton get such a high score on the quiz?

Bartholomew: Beats me.
Reginald: Because he got the bone-us question.

❖ ❖ ❖

Reginald: Why did grandma put roller skates on her rocking chair?
Bartholomew: I can't guess.
Reginald: Because she wanted to rock and roll.

❖ ❖ ❖

Reginald: Why did the chicken cross the road?
Bartholomew: I have no idea.
Reginald: To get to the other side.

❖ ❖ ❖

Reginald: Why do parents give their kids middle names?
Bartholomew: You tell me.
Reginald: So the kids will know when they are in trouble.

❖ ❖ ❖

Reginald: Why did the cheetah have spots?
Bartholomew: I give up.
Reginald: So everyone else could spot him.

❖ ❖ ❖

Reginald: Why did the dragon breathe on the village?
Bartholomew: Who knows?
Reginald: Because he wanted to eat the toast of the town.

❖ ❖ ❖

Reginald: Why did the plum take the prune to the dance?
Bartholomew: You've got me.
Reginald: Because he couldn't find a date.

❖ ❖ ❖

Reginald: Why is the school yard larger at recess?
Bartholomew: My mind is blank.
Reginald: Because there are more feet in it.

❖ ❖ ❖

Reginald: Why did the baker close the bakery?
Bartholomew: That's a mystery.
Reginald: Because she didn't make enough dough.

❖ ❖ ❖

Reginald: Why did the skunk sleep next to a ruler?
Bartholomew: I'm blank.
Reginald: To see how long he slept!

❖ ❖ ❖

Reginald: Why didn't the golfer wear two shoes?
Bartholomew: I don't have the foggiest.
Reginald: Because he had a hole in one.

❖ ❖ ❖

Reginald: Why did the man sleep under the oil tank?
Bartholomew: It's unknown to me.
Reginald: He wanted to get up oily in the morning.

❖ ❖ ❖

Reginald: Why did the turkey cross the road?
Bartholomew: I'm in the dark.
Reginald: Because it was the chicken's day off.

❖ ❖ ❖

Reginald: Why was the baby strawberry sad?
Bartholomew: Search me.
Reginald: Because its mommy was in a jam.

❖ ❖ ❖

Reginald: Why did Silly Billy bring a ladder to
school?
Bartholomew: You've got me guessing.
Reginald: Because he wanted to go to high
school.

❖ ❖ ❖

Reginald: Why was the baby dollar crying?
Bartholomew: I have no clue.
Reginald: It needed to be changed.

❖ ❖ ❖

Reginald: Why don't doctors feel queasy on
boats?
Bartholomew: I don't know.
Reginald: Because they're accustomed to see
sickness.

11

Tami & Tiffany

Tami: What's yellow and writes?
Tiffany: I have no clue.
Tami: A ballpoint banana.

❖ ❖ ❖

Tami: What cup can't you drink from?
Tiffany: I don't know.
Tami: A hiccup!

❖ ❖ ❖

Tami: What kind of shoe does a snake wear?
Tiffany: I can't guess.
Tami: Snakers.

❖ ❖ ❖

Tami: What is a snake's favorite subject in
   school?
Tiffany: I have no idea.
Tami: Hiss-tory!

❖ ❖ ❖

Tami: What did the dog say to the flea?
Tiffany: You tell me.
Tami: Don't bug me.

❖ ❖ ❖

Tami: Why was the piano laughing?
Tiffany: You tell me.
Tami: Someone kept tickling its keys.

❖ ❖ ❖

Tami: What did one knife say to the other knife?
Tiffany: Who knows?
Tami: You're looking sharp today.

❖ ❖ ❖

Tami: What did the teddy bear say when it was
   offered dessert?
Tiffany: You've got me.

Tami: No thanks. I'm stuffed.

❖ ❖ ❖

Tami: What did the porcupine say to the cactus?
Tiffany: My mind is blank.
Tami: Is that you, momma?

❖ ❖ ❖

Tami: Why are animal trainers well liked?
Tiffany: I give up.
Tami: They tame to please.

❖ ❖ ❖

Tami: What did the daddy rope say to the baby rope?
Tiffany: I'm blank.
Tami: Don't be knotty.

❖ ❖ ❖

Tami: Where do the smartest parrots live?
Tiffany: You tell me.
Tami: In the tropical brain forest.

12

Wanda & Adeline

Wanda: Why did the baby cross the road?
Adeline: I have no clue.
Wanda: It was the chicken's day off.

❖ ❖ ❖

Wanda: Why was the little drop of ink crying?
Adeline: I don't know.
Wanda: Because its mom was in the pen and he
  didn't know how long the sentence would be.

❖ ❖ ❖

Wanda: Why was the tomato red?
Adeline: Beats me.

Wanda: Because it saw the salad dressing.

❖ ❖ ❖

Wanda: Why did the elephant stand on the
marshmallow?
Adeline: I can't guess.
Wanda: So he wouldn't fall in the hot chocolate.

❖ ❖ ❖

Wanda: Why was the garbage feeling so sad?
Adeline: I have no idea.
Wanda: Because it was down in the dumps.

❖ ❖ ❖

Wanda: Why don't bears wear shoes?
Adeline: You tell me.
Wanda: Because then they wouldn't have bear
feet.

❖ ❖ ❖

Wanda: Why did the students eat their
English lesson?
Adeline: I give up.
Wanda: Because their teacher said it was a
piece of cake.

❖ ❖ ❖

Wanda: Why should you never iron your four-leaf clover?
Adeline: Who knows?
Wanda: Because you shouldn't press your luck.

❖ ❖ ❖

Wanda: Why did the girl sleep with her glasses on?
Adeline: You've got me.
Wanda: She wanted to see her dreams clearly.

❖ ❖ ❖

Wanda: Why did the reporter take a spoon with her?
Adeline: My mind is blank.
Wanda: She wanted a big scoop!

❖ ❖ ❖

Wanda: Why did the angel go to the hospital?
Adeline: That's a mystery.
Wanda: She had harp trouble.

❖ ❖ ❖

Wanda: Why can't a bicycle stand by itself?

Adeline: I'm blank.
Wanda: Because it is two tired.

❖ ❖ ❖

Wanda: Why did people think dinosaurs never slept?
Adeline: I don't have the foggiest.
Wanda: Because they never heard a dino-snore.

❖ ❖ ❖

Wanda: Why are movie stars such cool people?
Adeline: It's unknown to me.
Wanda: Because they have so many fans.

❖ ❖ ❖

Wanda: Why did the boy throw a piece of butter in the air
Adeline: I'm in the dark.
Wanda: Because he wanted to see a butter-fly!

13

Rudolf & Wilbur

Rudolf: What did they call Old MacDonald when he joined the army?
Wilbur: I have no clue.
Rudolf: G-I-G-I Joe.

❖ ❖ ❖

Rudolf: What do you call a man who shaves 20 times a day?
Wilbur: I don't know.
Rudolf: A barber.

❖ ❖ ❖

Rudolf: What skates wear out fast?

Wilbur: Beats me.
Rudolf: Cheapskates.

❖ ❖ ❖

Rudolf: What kind of markets do dogs hate?
Wilbur: I can't guess.
Rudolf: Flea markets.

❖ ❖ ❖

Rudolf: What do you get when you cross a parrot with a gorilla?
Wilbur: I have no idea.
Rudolf: A monster that says, "Polly wants a banana—now!"

❖ ❖ ❖

Rudolf: What do you call a dog with no legs?
Wilbur: You tell me.
Rudolf: Don't bother because he won't come anyway.

❖ ❖ ❖

Rudolf: What's the hardest foot to buy a skate for?
Wilbur: I give up.
Rudolf: A square foot.

❖ ❖ ❖

Rudolf: Why do elephants have short tails?
Wilbur: Who knows?
Rudolf: So they won't get caught in subway
   doors.

❖ ❖ ❖

Rudolf: What did Ben Franklin say when he
   discovered electricity?
Wilbur: You've got me.
Rudolf: Nothing. He was in shock.

❖ ❖ ❖

Rudolf: What room has no walls?
Wilbur: My mind is blank.
Rudolf: A mushroom.

❖ ❖ ❖

Rudolf: What did the refrigerator say to the
   microwave?
Wilbur: That's a mystery.
Rudolf: Salute me, I'm General Electric.

❖ ❖ ❖

Rudolf: What do you call a stupid robot?
Wilbur: I'm blank.
Rudolf: A dumbot.

❖ ❖ ❖

Rudolf: What do you call a monk who eats chips?
Wilbur: I don't have the foggiest.
Rudolf: A chip-monk.

❖ ❖ ❖

Rudolf: What do you get when you cross a sheep with a sandwich?
Wilbur: It's unknown to me.
Rudolf: Baa-loney!

❖ ❖ ❖

Rudolf: Where do mountains cook their food?
Wilbur: I give up.
Rudolf: On mountain ranges!

14

Christy & Clara

Christy: Where do you find a kid who keeps forgetting to clean his room?
Clara: I have no clue.
Christy: In hot water.

❖ ❖ ❖

Christy: Where does a baseball player live?
Clara: Beats me.
Christy: At home.

❖ ❖ ❖

Christy: Where did extinct animals go for the summer months?

Clara: I have no idea.
Christy: To the dino-shore.

❖ ❖ ❖

Christy: Where do people who are in a hurry live?
Clara: You tell me.
Christy: Mount Rushmore.

❖ ❖ ❖

Christy: Where do fish wash themselves?
Clara: I give up.
Christy: In a bass-tub.

❖ ❖ ❖

Christy: Where does a frog hang his coat?
Clara: Who knows?
Christy: In the croak room.

❖ ❖ ❖

Christy: Where do you find a missing snow-man?
Clara: You've got me.
Christy: The frost and found.

❖ ❖ ❖

Christy: Where does a dog go when it loses its tail?
Clara: My mind is blank.
Christy: To a re-tail shop.

❖ ❖ ❖

Christy: Where was the Declaration of Independence signed?
Clara: That's a mystery.
Christy: At the bottom.

❖ ❖ ❖

Christy: Where do you take a sick pony?
Clara: I'm blank.
Christy: To the horse-pital.

❖ ❖ ❖

Christy: Where does a computer keep its money?
Clara: I have no idea.
Christy: In its memory bank.

15

Ferdinand & Derek

Ferdinand: Where do fish sleep?
Derek: I have no clue.
Ferdinand: In water beds!

❖ ❖ ❖

Ferdinand: Where do Russian cows live?
Ferdinand: Beats me.
Ferdinand: In Moos-cow!

❖ ❖ ❖

Ferdinand: Where does a duck go when he's
    sick?
Derek: I can't guess.
Ferdinand: To the duck-tor.

❖   ❖   ❖

Ferdinand: Where do cars go to have fun?
Derek: I have no idea.
Ferdinand: A car-nival!

❖   ❖   ❖

Ferdinand: Where do cows go for their honey-moon?
Derek: You tell me.
Ferdinand: Cow-lifornia.

❖   ❖   ❖

Ferdinand: Where can you find flying rabbits?
Derek: I give up.
Ferdinand: In the hare-force.

❖   ❖   ❖

Ferdinand: Where do monkeys go to work out?
Derek: Who knows?
Ferdinand: To the jungle gym.

❖   ❖   ❖

Ferdinand: Where do cars get the most flat tires?

Derek: You've got me.
Ferdinand: At the fork in the road.

❖ ❖ ❖

Ferdinand: Where do kings get crowned?
Derek: My mind is blank.
Ferdinand: On their heads.

❖ ❖ ❖

Ferdinand: Where is the best place to find terrified woodpeckers?
Derek: I can't guess.
Ferdinand: In a petrified forest.

16

Stop That Knocking!

Knock, knock.
Who's there?
You.
You who?
Hey, you who yourself.

❖   ❖   ❖

Knock, knock.
Who's there?
Iben.
Iben who?
Iben a good boy.

❖   ❖   ❖

Knock, knock.
Who's there?
Canoe.
Canoe who?
Canoe come out and play?

❖   ❖   ❖

Knock, knock.
Who's there?
Lettuce.
Lettuce who?
Lettuce go see the movie.

❖   ❖   ❖

Knock, knock.
Who's there?
Midas.
Midas who?
Midas well open the door and find out.

17

Gertrude & Doris

Gertrude: Which is faster, heat or cold?
Doris: I have no clue.
Gertrude: Heat. You can catch a cold.

❖ ❖ ❖

Gertrude: Who never does a day's work but gets
paid anyway?
Doris: I don't know.
Gertrude: A night watchman.

❖ ❖ ❖

Gertrude: Which baseball player makes the
best pancakes?

Doris: Beats me.
Gertrude: The batter.

❖ ❖ ❖

Gertrude: Who was the biggest monarch in history?
Doris: I can't guess.
Gertrude: King Kong.

❖ ❖ ❖

Gertrude: Who wrote "Oh say can you see?"
Doris: I have no idea.
Gertrude: An eye doctor.

❖ ❖ ❖

Gertrude: Which midwestern state has two eyes but cannot see?
Doris: You tell me.
Gertrude: Indiana.

❖ ❖ ❖

Gertrude: Who has the loudest voice?
Doris: I give up.
Gertrude: The I-scream man.

❖ ❖ ❖

Gertrude: Who can jump higher than a house?
Doris: Who knows?
Gertrude: Anyone. Houses can't jump.

❖ ❖ ❖

Gertrude: Which is heavier—a full moon or a half moon?
Doris: You've got me.
Gertrude: The full moon is lighter.

❖ ❖ ❖

Gertrude: Who's your best friend at school?
Doris: My mind is blank.
Gertrude: Your princi-pal.

❖ ❖ ❖

Gertrude: When should a baker stop making doughnuts?
Doris: That's a mystery.
Gertrude: When he gets tired of the hole business.

Gertrude: When an ant looks at his family tree, what does he see?
Doris: I'm blank.
Gertrude: His ant-cestors.

❖   ❖   ❖

Gertrude: Who is the strongest man in the world?
Doris: I don't have the foggiest.
Gertrude: The policeman. He can hold up cars with one hand.

❖   ❖   ❖

Gertrude: Do you know what kind of tree grows in your hand?
Doris: It's unknown to me.
Gertrude: A palm tree.

18

Tony & Todd

Tony: What do you get when you cross a rooster with a poodle?
Todd: I have no clue.
Tony: A cock-a-poodle-doo.

❖ ❖ ❖

Tony: What happens when you don't dust your mirror?
Todd: I don't know.
Tony: It gives you a dirty look.

❖ ❖ ❖

Tony: What do you call a two-ton bear?

Todd: Beats me.
Tony: Sir.

❖ ❖ ❖

Tony: What side dish do coal miners eat at lunch?
Todd: I can't guess.
Tony: Coalslaw.

❖ ❖ ❖

Tony: What's black and white and red all over?
Todd: I have no idea.
Tony: An embarrassed penguin.

❖ ❖ ❖

Tony: What did the man say when he lost his dog?
Todd: You tell me.
Tony: Dog-gone.

❖ ❖ ❖

Tony: What kind of fruit can you drink from a straw?
Todd: I give up.
Tony: A straw-berry.

❖ ❖ ❖

Tony: What has eight wheels but only one passenger?
Todd: Who knows?
Tony: A pair of in-line skates.

❖ ❖ ❖

Tony: What is the biggest pencil in the world?
Todd: You've got me.
Tony: Pennsylvania.

19

Ryan & Randy

Ryan: How do you start a lightning bug race?
Randy: I have no clue.
Ryan: Ready, set, glow!

❖ ❖ ❖

Ryan: How do you count cows?
Randy: I don't know.
Ryan: With a cow-culator.

❖ ❖ ❖

Ryan: How much dirt is in a hole one foot wide
and one foot deep?
Randy: Beats me.

Ryan: None. There is no dirt in a hole.

❖　❖　❖

Ryan: How many dogs does it take to make a winter coat?
Randy: I can't guess.
Ryan: Zero. Dogs can't sew.

❖　❖　❖

Ryan: How do you make the word "one" disappear?
Randy: I have no idea.
Randy: Put a "g" in front of it and its "gone."

❖　❖　❖

Ryan: How do messy students write their reports?
Randy: You tell me.
Ryan: With their pig-pens.

❖　❖　❖

Ryan: How did the bear make the hotdog shiver?
Randy: I give up.
Ryan: He covered it with chili beans.

❖ ❖ ❖

Ryan: How do robins get into shape?
Randy: Who knows?
Ryan: They do worm-ups.

❖ ❖ ❖

Ryan: How far can you see in a lettuce patch?
Randy: You've got me.
Ryan: Not far at all—there are too many heads
in the way.

❖ ❖ ❖

Ryan: How do books keep warm?
Randy: My mind is blank.
Ryan: They have jackets.

❖ ❖ ❖

Ryan: How is the plot of a mystery like
making pudding?
Randy: That's a puzzle.
Ryan: They both thicken as you go along.

❖ ❖ ❖

Ryan: How do you know which end of a worm is
the head?
Randy: I'm blank.
Ryan: You tickle it in the middle and see which
end laughs.

❖ ❖ ❖

Ryan: How do you keep a skunk from smelling?
Randy: I don't have the foggiest.
Ryan: Hold its nose.

❖ ❖ ❖

Ryan: How do you stop a bull from charging?
Randy: It's unknown to me.
Ryan: Take away his credit card.

❖ ❖ ❖

Ryan: How do you make a chocolate shake?
Randy: I'm in the dark.
Ryan: Take it to a scary movie.

❖ ❖ ❖

Ryan: How do you catch a unique rabbit?
Randy: Search me.
Ryan: Unique up on him.

❖ ❖ ❖

Ryan: How can you tell if a tree is a dogwood
  tree?
Randy: You've got me guessing.
Ryan: By its bark.

20

Henrietta & Ruby

Henrietta: How are an island and the letter **T** alike?

Ruby: I have no clue.

Herietta: They are both in the middle of water.

❖ ❖ ❖

Henrietta: How do you make money?

Ruby: I don't know.

Henrietta: Make yourself a sandwich and cut it into four quarters.

❖ ❖ ❖

Henrietta: How do you stop a mouse from squeaking?
Ruby: Beats me.
Henrietta: Oil it!

❖ ❖ ❖

Henrietta: How do you spell mousetrap with 3 letters?
Ruby: I can't guess.
Henrietta: C - A - T.

❖ ❖ ❖

Henrietta: How do you make gold soup?
Ruby: I have no idea.
Henrietta: Add fourteen carats.

❖ ❖ ❖

Henrietta: How did the sheriff find the missing barber?
Ruby: You tell me.
Henrietta: He combed the town.

❖ ❖ ❖

Henrietta: How do you congratulate a champion octopus?
Ruby: I give up.

Henrietta: You shake his hand, hand, hand, hand, hand, hand, hand, hand.

❖ ❖ ❖

Henrietta: How many sides does a bowling ball have?
Ruby: Who knows?
Henrietta: Just two—inside and outside.

❖ ❖ ❖

Henrietta: How do you start a flea race?
Ruby: You've got me.
Henrietta: One, two, flea, go!

21

Hubert & Erastus

Hubert: What's the only weather you can eat?
Erastus: I have no clue.
Hubert: Chili.

❖ ❖ ❖

Hubert: What did the boy banana say to the girl banana?
Erastus: I don't know.
Hubert: You're very a-peeling.

❖ ❖ ❖

Hubert: Why did it take so long for the elephant to cross the road?

Erastus: You've got me.
Hubert: Because the chicken had trouble car-
rying him!

❖ ❖ ❖

Hubert: What do you call a place where mon-
sters live?
Erastus: I can't guess.
Hubert: A terror-tory.

❖ ❖ ❖

Hubert: What do you get when you cross a
chicken with a bell?
Erastus: I have no idea.
Hubert: An alarm cluck.

❖ ❖ ❖

Hubert: What goes all around the yard but
never moves?
Erastus: You tell me.
Hubert: A fence.

❖ ❖ ❖

Hubert: What do you call a turtle with a box?
Erastus: I give up.
Hubert: A box turtle.

❖ ❖ ❖

Hubert: What goes up a hill and down a hill, but never moves?
Erastus: Who knows?
Hubert: A road.

❖ ❖ ❖

Hubert: What is easy to get into but hard to get out of?
Erastus: You've got me.
Hubert: Trouble.

❖ ❖ ❖

Hubert: What has two heads, six legs, one tail, four eyes, two arms, and one hat?
Erastus: My mind is blank.
Hubert: A man on a horse.

❖ ❖ ❖

Hubert: What book has the most people in it?
Erastus: That's a mystery.
Hubert: The telephone book.

❖ ❖ ❖

Hubert: What did the corn say to his doctor?
Erastus: I'm blank.
Hubert: I have an earache.

❖ ❖ ❖

Hubert: What month has 27 days?
Erastus: I don't have the foggiest.
Hubert: All of them.

❖ ❖ ❖

Hubert: What do you get when you cross a duck
with a pumpkin?
Erastus: It's unknown to me.
Hubert: A quack-a-lantern.

❖ ❖ ❖

Hubert: What did the boy volcano say to the girl
volcano?
Erastus: I'm in the dark.
Hubert: Do you lava me like I lava you?

❖ ❖ ❖

Hubert: What do you get when you cross a four
leaf clover with poison ivy?
Erastus: Search me.
Hubert: A rash of good luck.

22

Myrtle & Winifred

Myrtle: What do you call a crocodile that enjoys bowling?
Winifred: I have no clue.
Myrtle: An alley-gator.

❖   ❖   ❖

Myrtle: What did the necktie say to the hat?
Winifred: I don't know.
Myrtle: You go on a head, and I'll just hang around here for a while.

❖   ❖   ❖

Myrtle: What goes up when the rain comes down?

Winifred: Beats me.
Myrtle: An umbrella.

❖ ❖ ❖

Myrtle: Why are rivers rich?
Winifred: My mind is blank.
Myrtle: Every river has two banks.

❖ ❖ ❖

Myrtle: What kind of jam can't go on bread?
Winifred: I have no idea.
Myrtle: A traffic jam.

❖ ❖ ❖

Myrtle: What does a bee use to fix its hair?
Winifred: You tell me.
Myrtle: A honeycomb!

❖ ❖ ❖

Myrtle: What do you get when you cross a frog
   with a potato?
Winifred: I give up.
Myrtle: A potatoad!

❖ ❖ ❖

Myrtle: What kind of driver never gets a ticket?
Winifred: Who knows?
Myrtle: A screwdriver.

❖ ❖ ❖

Myrtle: What did the chimpanzee say when his
sister had a baby?
Winifred: You've got me.
Myrtle: Well, I'll be a monkey's uncle.

❖ ❖ ❖

Myrtle: What is the weather report?
Winifred: My mind is blank.
Myrtle: Chili today, hot tamale.

❖ ❖ ❖

Myrtle: What is green and smells like paint?
Winifred: That's a mystery.
Myrtle: Green paint.

❖ ❖ ❖

Myrtle: What do you call two spiders who just
got married?
Winifred: I'm blank.
Myrtle: Newlywebs.

❖ ❖ ❖

Myrtle: What did the mountain say to the earthquake?
Winifred: I don't have the foggiest.
Myrtle: It's not my fault!

❖ ❖ ❖

Myrtle: What do you do when a snake is in your bed?
Winifred: It's unknown to me.
Myrtle: Sleep on the dresser.

❖ ❖ ❖

Myrtle: What state should you jump rope in?
Winifred: I'm in the dark.
Myrtle: New Hemp-shire.

❖ ❖ ❖

Myrtle: What dinosaur loves vegetables?
Winifred: Search me.
Myrtle: A broccoli-saurus.

❖ ❖ ❖

Myrtle: What ten letter word starts with gas?
Winifred: You've got me guessing.
Myrtle: Automobile.

❖ ❖ ❖

Myrtle: What's the hardest part of taking a test?
Winifred: I pass.
Myrtle: The answers.

❖ ❖ ❖

Myrtle: What loses its head in the morning and gets it back at night?
Winifred: How should I know?
Myrtle: A pillow.

23

Jon-Mark & Julius

Jon-Mark: What kind of birds hang around ski slopes?
Julius: I have no clue.
Jon-Mark: Ski gulls.

❖ ❖ ❖

Jon-Mark: What kind of fish is a household pet?
Julius: I don't know.
Jon-Mark: A catfish!

❖ ❖ ❖

Jon-Mark: What did the mother sheep say to her baby?

Julius: Beats me.
Jon-Mark: Don't be baaaaaad.

❖ ❖ ❖

Jon-Mark: Why did the doctor operate on the
book?
Julius: That's a mystery.
Jon-Mark: He wanted to remove its appendix.

❖ ❖ ❖

Jon-Mark: What animal has two trunks?
Julius: I have no idea.
Jon-Mark: An elephant going swimming.

❖ ❖ ❖

Jon-Mark: What has four legs and is green,
white, and black?
Julius: You tell me.
Jon-Mark: A cow that just got off a roller
coaster.

❖ ❖ ❖

Jon-Mark: What's black and white and hops?
Julius: I give up.
Jon-Mark: A panda on a pogo stick.

❖ ❖ ❖

Jon-Mark: What can you make with two banana peels?
Julius: Who knows?
Jon-Mark: A pair of slippers.

❖ ❖ ❖

Jon-Mark: What's green and crawls on all fours?
Julius: You've got me.
Jon-Mark: A girl scout who dropped her cookies.

❖ ❖ ❖

Jon-Mark: What do you get when you cross two chickens and two bombs?
Julius: My mind is blank.
Jon-Mark: A chicka-chicka boom boom!

❖ ❖ ❖

Jon-Mark: What's the difference between a coyote and a flea?
Julius: That's a mystery.
Jon-Mark: One howls on the prairie; the other prowls on the hairy.

❖   ❖   ❖

Jon-Mark: What goes boing, boing, boing, splat?
Julius: I'm blank.
Jon-Mark: A grasshopper crossing a busy road.

24

Edna & Agnes

Edna: What do you get when you cross an electric eel and a sponge?
Agnes: I have no clue.
Edna: A shock absorber.

❖ ❖ ❖

Edna: What would happen if everyone in the country painted their car red?
Agnes: I don't know.
Edna: We would have a red car-nation.

❖ ❖ ❖

Edna: What has four wheels and flies?

Agnes: Beats me.
Edna: A garbage truck.

❖ ❖ ❖

Edna: What has four wheels, a tongue, and a body?
Agnes: I can't guess.
Edna: A wagon.

❖ ❖ ❖

Edna: What fruit can change itself into a vegetable?
Agnes: I have no idea.
Edna: A tomato—you can throw it up in the air and it will come down squash!

❖ ❖ ❖

Edna: What's white and goes up?
Agnes: You tell me.
Edna: A confused snowflake.

❖ ❖ ❖

Edna: What do you get if you cross a lunch box and a school book?
Agnes: I give up.

Edna: Food for thought.

❖ ❖ ❖

Edna: What kind of bean doesn't grow in a vegetable garden?
Agnes: Who knows?
Edna: A jelly bean.

❖ ❖ ❖

Edna: What did the ocean say to the ship?
Agnes: My mind is blank.
Edna: Nothing, it just waved.

❖ ❖ ❖

Edna: What is cold and rings?
Agnes: That's a mystery.
Edna: An ice-cream phone.

❖ ❖ ❖

Edna: What do you get when you plant kisses?
Agnes: I'm blank.
Edna: Two lips.

❖ ❖ ❖

Edna: What does a mermaid sleep on when she goes to bed at night?
Agnes: I don't have the foggiest.
Edna: A waterbed.

❖   ❖   ❖

Edna: What does one banana say to another banana when they're in trouble?
Agnes: It's unknown to me.
Edna: Let's split!

❖   ❖   ❖

Edna: What kind of girl does a hamburger like?
Agnes: I'm in the dark.
Edna: Any girl named "Patty."

❖   ❖   ❖

Edna: What did the baby light bulb say to its mother?
Agnes: Search me.
Edna: I wuv you watts and watts.

25

Ambrose & Abner

Ambrose: What do you get when you squeeze a
curtain?
Abner: I have no clue.
Ambrose: Drape juice.

❖ ❖ ❖

Ambrose: What do mice like to drink in the
summer?
Abner: I don't know.
Ambrose: Mice Tea.

❖ ❖ ❖

Ambrose: What is the most important part of a
horse?

Abner: Beats me.
Ambrose: The mane part.

❖   ❖   ❖

Ambrose: What has four eyes and sleeps in a water bed?
Abner: I can't guess.
Ambrose: The Mississippi.

❖   ❖   ❖

Ambrose: What kind of car does a cow drive?
Abner: I have no idea.
Ambrose: A cattlelac.

❖   ❖   ❖

Ambrose: What does humdrum mean?
Abner: You tell me.
Ambrose: It's what a drummer does when he forgets his sticks.

❖   ❖   ❖

Ambrose: What do cowboys like on their pancakes?
Abner: I give up.
Ambrose: Maple stirrup.

❖ ❖ ❖

Ambrose: What do you get when you cross
  Lassie and a pit bull?
Abner: You've got me.
Ambrose: A dog who will chew your legs off,
  then run for help.

26

Kati & Kimberly

Kati: If you had 50 seconds to live and 50 cents, what would you buy?
Kimberly: I have no clue.
Kati: LifeSavers.

❖ ❖ ❖

Kati: If there are seven people and one dog under one tiny umbrella, why didn't anyone get wet?
Kimberly: I don't know.
Kati: It wasn't raining.

❖ ❖ ❖

Kati: Mr. Green is a butcher. He is six feet tall and wears a size 40 suit. What does he weigh?
Kimberly: Beats me.
Kati: Meat.

❖ ❖ ❖

Kati: If April showers bring May flowers, what do May flowers bring?
Kimberly: I can't guess.
Kati: Pilgrims.

❖ ❖ ❖

Kati: Wanna hear a clean joke?
Kimberly: Okay.
Kati: A horse jumped in the water.

❖ ❖ ❖

Kati: Did you hear about the guy who walked into the bar?
Kimberly: No, what happened?
Kati: He said, *"Ouch!"*

❖ ❖ ❖

Kati: I can make words disappear, and the more you use me, the smaller I become. What am I?

Kimberly: I give up.
Kati: An eraser.

❖   ❖   ❖

Kati: Did you hear the joke about the peach?
Kimberly: No, what is it?
Kati: It's pit-i-ful.

❖   ❖   ❖

Kati: Did you hear about the boxer who didn't like to jump rope?
Kimberly: Not yet.
Kati: Skip it.

❖   ❖   ❖

Kati: Did you hear the joke about the 50 foot giant?
Kimberly: My mind is blank.
Kati: Never mind, it's way over your head.

❖   ❖   ❖

Kati: What holiday do buffalo celebrate?
Kimberly: That's a mystery.
Kati: Bison-tennial day.

❖   ❖   ❖

Kati: What did one arithmetic book say to the other arithmetic book?
Kimberly: I'm blank.
Kati: Boy, do I have problems.

27

Amanda & Allison

Amanda: What's the difference between a
watchman and a jeweler?
Allison: I have no clue.
Amanda: One watches and the other sells
watches.

❖ ❖ ❖

Amanda: What kind of bird sits on a stool?
Allison: I don't know.
Amanda: A stool pigeon.

❖ ❖ ❖

Amanda: What do you call a cow with no legs?

Allison: Beats me.
Amanda: Ground beef.

❖ ❖ ❖

Amanda: Why did the door get fired?
Allison: I don't have the foggiest.
Amanda: It was lying down on the knob.

❖ ❖ ❖

Amanda: What did the digital clock say to its
mother?
Allison: I have no idea.
Amanda: Look Mom, no hands!

❖ ❖ ❖

Amanda: What did one wall say to the other
wall?
Allison: You tell me.
Amanda: I'll meet you in the corner.

❖ ❖ ❖

Amanda: What is the strongest small animal?
Allison: I give up.
Amanda: A snail, because it carries its house on
its back.

❖ ❖ ❖

Amanda: What kind of cap does a car wear?
Allison: Who knows?
Amanda: A hubcap.

❖ ❖ ❖

Amanda: What starts with a "P," ends with an "E," and has a million letters in between?
Allison: You've got me.
Amanda: The post office.

❖ ❖ ❖

Amanda: What did the farmer say when he lost his sheep?
Allison: My mind is blank.
Amanda: Help! I've lost my sheep!

❖ ❖ ❖

Amanda: What has 20 heads but can't think?
Allison: That's a mystery.
Amanda: A book of matches.

❖ ❖ ❖

Amanda: What did one elevator say to the other elevator?

Allison: I'm blank.
Amanda: I'm moving up in life.

❖ ❖ ❖

Amanda: Why won't weathermen tell each
other jokes?
Allison: It's unknown to me.
Amanda: They don't want to laugh up a
storm.

28

Zachary & Sophia

Zachary: What did the carpet say to the floor?
Sophia: I have no clue.
Zachary: I've got you covered.

❖ ❖ ❖

Zachary: What did the farmer say when he
lost his tractor?
Sophia: I don't know.
Zachary: Where's my tractor?

❖ ❖ ❖

Zachary: What did the paper say to the scis-
sors?

Sophia: Beats me.
Zachary: Cut it out!

❖ ❖ ❖

Zachary: What's a knight's favorite fish?
Sophia: I can't guess.
Zachary: Swordfish.

❖ ❖ ❖

Zachary: What do you call a dog with no legs that sits in front of somebody's door?
Sophia: I have no idea.
Zachary: Matt.

❖ ❖ ❖

Zachary: What did the horse say when he was asked to jump into the water?
Sophia: You tell me.
Zachary: Neigh.

❖ ❖ ❖

Zachary: What happens when you swallow a nuclear bomb?
Sophia: I give up.
Zachary: You get atomic-ache.

❖ ❖ ❖

Zachary: What goes up and never comes down?
Sophia: You've got me.
Zachary: Your age.

❖ ❖ ❖

Zachary: Why wouldn't the ewe kiss the ram?
Sophia: I'm in the dark.
Zachary: He had baa breath.

❖ ❖ ❖

Zachary: What do you get when you cross a lawnmower and a cow?
Sophia: That's a mystery.
Zachary: A lawnmooer.

❖ ❖ ❖

Zachary: What kind of horses frighten ranchers?
Sophia: I'm blank.
Zachary: Nightmares.

❖ ❖ ❖

Zachary: What did the judge say when a skunk entered the courtroom?
Sophia: I don't have the foggiest.
Zachary: Odor in the court.

❖   ❖   ❖

Zachary: What two letters tell you it's time to stop for gas?
Sophia: It's unknown to me.
Zachary: M-T.

29

Odds & Ends

Mom: Son, you've got your shoes on the wrong feet.

Son: Then whose feet are they supposed to be on?

❖ ❖ ❖

Emily: There was this rooster who laid an egg on the roof of a barn, which way do you think it rolled?

Lacey: Beats me.

Emily: Roosters don't lay eggs!

❖ ❖ ❖

A king on a tropical island was given a new throne. He took his old one and stored it in the attic of his grass hut. He kept on getting new thrones from people in the village, and each time he would store the old one in his attic. Finally the attic collapsed and the king was killed.

Moral: People who live in grass huts shouldn't stow thrones.

Patient: I went to my psychiatrist and told him that I'm going crazy. One night I dreamed I was a wigwam. The next night I dreamed I was a teepee.

Psychiatrist: I know what your problem is. You're too tents!

One time a big shot gangster decided to pay a man named Artie $1.00 to choke a man in a hotel room. After choking him, Artie heard the maid come in, so he choked her, too—but not before she screamed.

Hearing the scream, the hotel owner ran in to see what was going on. He was barely able to dial 911 before Artie choked him also.

When the police arrived, they caught Artie.
The next day the newspaper headline read,
"Artie chokes 3 for $1.00."

30

Boris & Bruno

Boris: Why does a dog wag its tail?
Bruno: I have no clue.
Boris: Because no one else will wag it for him.

❖　❖　❖

Boris: Why do so many elephants wear bright-green nail polish?
Bruno: Beats me.
Boris: So they can hide in the pea patch.

❖　❖　❖

Boris: Why did Mother Cobra put powder on her babies?

Bruno: You tell me.
Boris: To avoid viper rash.

❖ ❖ ❖

Boris: Why did the teacher send the chicken to the principal's office?
Bruno: I give up.
Boris: Because it kept pecking on the other kids.

❖ ❖ ❖

Boris: Why is a bride sad on her wedding day?
Bruno: Who knows?
Boris: She doesn't get to marry the best man.

❖ ❖ ❖

Boris: Why don't grapes ever get lonely?
Bruno: You've got me.
Boris: They hang around in bunches.

❖ ❖ ❖

Boris: Why does the sun get so big just before it goes down?
Bruno: My mind is blank.
Boris: It has sucked up all the daylight.

❖ ❖ ❖

Boris: Why did the moth eat a hole in the rug?
Bruno: That's a mystery.
Boris: He wanted to see the floor show.

❖ ❖ ❖

Boris: Why did the farmer buy so much land?
Bruno: I'm blank.
Boris: He got it dirt cheap.

❖ ❖ ❖

Boris: Why does an elephant wear glasses?
Bruno: I don't have the foggiest.
Boris: So he can read all of these great riddles!

❖ ❖ ❖

Boris: Why isn't the elderly mayor getting reelected?
Bruno: It's unknown to me.
Boris: Because the old gray mayor just ain't what he used to be.

❖ ❖ ❖

Boris: Why did the boy quit looking for a Band-Aid?
Bruno: I'm in the dark.
Boris: It was a lost gauze.

31

Alfreda & Amelia

Alfreda: How did the ecologist feel when the trees turned to stone?
Amelia: I have no clue.
Alfreda: He was petrified.

Alfreda: How can a teacher tell if there's an elephant in the classroom?
Amelia: I don't know.
Alfreda: Ask a question; if someone raises a trunk instead of a hand, then there's an elephant in the classroom.

Alfreda: How does Miss Piggy travel to work?
Amelia: Beats me.
Alfreda: By Hamtrak.

❖ ❖ ❖

Alfreda: How did the ant get its reputation as a
hard worker?
Amelia: I can't guess.
Alfreda: It always has time to go to picnics.

❖ ❖ ❖

Alfreda: How do loudmouths pay for college?
Amelia: I have no idea.
Alfreda: They get hollerships.

❖ ❖ ❖

Alfreda: How do camels hide in the desert?
Amelia: You tell me.
Alfreda: They wear camel-flage.

❖ ❖ ❖

Alfreda: How do you turn a man into wood?
Amelia: I give up.
Alfreda: Put him on a ship and he'll be aboard.

❖ ❖ ❖

Alfreda: How do you make a kitchen sink?
Amelia: Who knows?
Alfreda: Throw it in the ocean.

❖ ❖ ❖

Alfreda: How would you describe a beaver, a frog, a pig, and a big fish?
Amelia: You've got me.
Alfreda: A chopper, a hopper, a slopper, and a whopper.

❖ ❖ ❖

Alfreda: Did you hear how Terry's horse farm turned out?
Amelia: No, tell me.
Alfreda: Not very good. He planted the horses too deep.

❖ ❖ ❖

Alfreda: How do acrobats fall in love?
Amelia: That's a mystery.
Alfreda: Head over heels.

❖ ❖ ❖

Alfreda: How can you tell if a lobster is fresh?
Amelia: I'm blank.
Alfreda: If he tries to kiss you.

❖   ❖   ❖

Alfreda: How do you hit slime?
Amelia: It's unknown to me.
Alfreda: With a sludgehammer.

❖   ❖   ❖

Alfreda: How did the police describe the hitch-hiker?
Amelia: I'm in the dark.
Alfreda: They gave a thumbnail description.

❖   ❖   ❖

Alfreda: How do baby birds learn how to fly?
Amelia: Search me.
Alfreda: They just sort of wing it.

32

Chauncey & Chester

Chauncey: What is round, flat, and makes a terrible racket?
Chester: I have no clue.
Chauncey: Tennis the Menace.

❖ ❖ ❖

Chauncey: What do you call a camel that lives in a garbage pit?
Chester: I don't know.
Chauncey: Humpty Dumpty.

❖ ❖ ❖

Chauncey: What's the best way to mail a pizza?

Chester: Beats me.
Chauncey: With food stamps.

❖ ❖ ❖

Chauncey: What would you get if you crossed an owl with a babysitter?
Chester: I can't guess.
Chauncey: A whoo-te-nanny.

❖ ❖ ❖

Chauncey: What color is a cheerleader?
Chester: I have no idea.
Chauncey: Yeller.

❖ ❖ ❖

Chauncey: What is the difference between a pig and a doughnut?
Chester: You tell me.
Chauncey: It's a lot more difficult to dunk a pig into your coffee.

❖ ❖ ❖

Chauncey: What has four legs, four arms, four eyes, four ears, two heads, two noses, and two mouths?

Chester: I give up.
Chauncey: A person with extra parts.

❖ ❖ ❖

Chauncey: What is black and white and yellow?
Chester: Who knows?
Chauncey: A bus full of zebras.

❖ ❖ ❖

Chauncey: What kind of monkey flies?
Chester: You've got me.
Chauncey: A hot-air baboon.

❖ ❖ ❖

Chauncey: What did the scientist say when they found bones on the moon?
Chester: My mind is blank.
Chauncey: The cow didn't make it.

❖ ❖ ❖

Chauncey: What kind of cake do policemen like?
Chester: That's a mystery.
Chauncey: Cop-cakes.

❖ ❖ ❖

Chauncey: What would you get if you crossed a
  nut and a briefcase.
Chester: I'm blank.
Chauncey: A nut-case.

❖ ❖ ❖

Chauncey: What do you call a sleeping bag?
Chester: I don't have the foggiest.
Chauncey: A knapsack.

❖ ❖ ❖

Chauncey: What did the man say when he saw
  the woman's terrible painting?
Chester: It's unknown to me.
Chauncey: I'm going to have an art attack.

33

Let Me In!

Knock, knock.
Who's there?
Police.
Police who?
Police let me in; it's cold out here.

Knock, knock.
Who's there?
Mabel.
Mabel who?
Mabel I'll tell you and Mabel I won't.

Knock, knock.
Who's there?
Wash Out.
Wash Out who?
Wash Out, I'm coming in.

Knock, knock.
Who's there?
Diplomas.
Diplomas who?
Diplomas here to fix your leaky pipes.

Knock, knock.
Who's there?
Wire.
Wire who?
Wire we telling knock-knock jokes?

❖ ❖ ❖

Knock, knock.
Who's there?
Wayne.
Wayne who?
Wayne, Wayne, go away, come again another day.

❖ ❖ ❖

Knock, knock.
Who's there?
Ivan.
Ivan who?
Ivan itch and I can't reach it. Will you scratch it
for me?

❖ ❖ ❖

Knock, knock.
Who's there?
Tommy.
Tommy who?
I have a tommy-ache!

❖ ❖ ❖

Knock, knock.
Who's there?
Annapolis.
Annapolis who?
Annapolis day keeps the doctor away.

34

Edwina & Effie

Edwina: What happened to the boy who ate a window?
Effie: I don't know.
Edwina: He got a pane in his stomach.

❖ ❖ ❖

Edwina: What do you call a bear who cries a lot?
Effie: Beats me.
Edwina: Winnie the Boo-hoo.

❖ ❖ ❖

Edwina: What do cats eat for breakfast?
Effie: I can't guess.
Edwina: Mice Krispies.

❖ ❖ ❖

Edwina: What do you get if you cross a centipede with a chicken?
Effie: I have no idea.
Edwina: Fewer fights over who gets the drumsticks.

❖ ❖ ❖

Edwina: What comes after Humphrey?
Effie: You tell me.
Edwina: Humph-four.

❖ ❖ ❖

Edwina: What does the invisible man call his mother and father?
Effie: Who knows?
Edwina: His transparents.

❖ ❖ ❖

Edwina: What became of the crossword addict who died?
Effie: You've got me.
Edwina: He was buried six feet down and three across.

❖ ❖ ❖

Edwina: What did the pencil say to the paper?
Effie: My mind is blank.
Edwina: I dot my i's on you.

❖ ❖ ❖

Edwina: What is a druggist's favorite song?
Effie: That's a mystery.
Edwina: Old MacDonald had a pharm-acy.

❖ ❖ ❖

Edwina: What would you get if you crossed a rooster with morning mist?
Effie: I'm blank.
Edwina: Cock-a-doodle-dew.

❖ ❖ ❖

Edwina: What do you get when you cross an owl with a skunk?
Effie: It's unknown to me.
Edwina: An owl that smells bad but doesn't give a hoot.

Edwina: What lies on the ground, 100 feet up in the air?
Effie: I'm in the dark.
Edwina: A dead centipede.

❖ ❖ ❖

Edwina: What do you get when the postman spills ink in his mail pouch?
Effie: Search me.
Edwina: Blackmail.

❖ ❖ ❖

Edwina: What kind of shirts do golfers wear?
Effie: I pass.
Edwina: Tee-shirts.

35

Dexter & Dudley

Dexter: What did the waiter do when he joined
the Army?
Dudley: I have no clue.
Dexter: He learned how to take orders.

❖ ❖ ❖

Dexter: What ship carries lots of rabbits?
Dudley: I don't know.
Dexter: A hare-craft carrier.

❖ ❖ ❖

Dexter: What animal lives at the North Pole
and scores strikes and spares?

Dudley: Beats me.
Dexter: A bowler bear.

❖ ❖ ❖

Dexter: What do you call a person who is broke
and stranded in the mall?
Dudley: I can't guess.
Dexter: Shopwrecked.

❖ ❖ ❖

Dexter: What do you call the celebration of 200
years of shopping?
Dudley: I have no idea.
Dexter: The buy-centennial.

❖ ❖ ❖

Dexter: What powerful reptile lives in the
Emerald City?
Dudley: You tell me.
Dexter: The Lizard of Oz.

❖ ❖ ❖

Dexter: What kind of paper makes you itch?
Dudley: I give up.
Dexter: Scratch paper.

❖ ❖ ❖

Dexter: What is a quarterback's favorite game?
Dudley: Who knows?
Dexter: Tic-Tackle-Toe.

❖ ❖ ❖

Dexter: What bear doesn't want to grow up?
Dudley: You've got me.
Dexter: Peter Panda.

❖ ❖ ❖

Dexter: What beats chasing a pig around the yard?
Dudley: My mind is blank.
Dexter: Your heart.

❖ ❖ ❖

Dexter: What does a baby snake play with?
Dudley: That's a mystery.
Dexter: A rattle.

❖ ❖ ❖

Dexter: What makes the floor of a basketball court all wet?

Dudley: I'm blank.
Dexter: The players—they dribble a lot.

❖ ❖ ❖

Dexter: What did the rake say to the hoe?
Dudley: It's unknown to me.
Dexter: Hi hoe.

36

Lena & Lulu

Lena: What do crocodiles drink before a big race?
Lulu: I have no clue.
Lena: Ali-Gatorade.

❖ ❖ ❖

Lena: What wild pig goes around stamping out forest fires?
Lulu: I don't know.
Lena: Smokey the Boar.

❖ ❖ ❖

Lena: What did the shrimp yell to the seaweed?

Lulu: Beats me.
Lena: Kelp! Kelp!

❖ ❖ ❖

Lena: What do turtles give each other for Christmas?
Lulu: I have no idea.
Lena: People-neck sweaters.

❖ ❖ ❖

Lena: What is orange and half a mile high?
Lulu: You tell me.
Lena: The Empire State Carrot.

❖ ❖ ❖

Lena: What do you get when you cross a parrot with an elephant?
Lulu: I give up.
Lena: An animal that tells what it remembers.

❖ ❖ ❖

Lena: What would you say to the hockey player that earns $1,000,000 a year?
Lulu: Who knows?
Lena: That's ice work, if you can get it.

❖ ❖ ❖

Lena: What is faster than a speeding bullet, more powerful than a locomotive, and green?
Lulu: You've got me.
Lena: Superpickle.

❖ ❖ ❖

Lena: What did the judge say when she got home from work?
Lulu: My mind is blank.
Lena: It's been a trying day.

❖ ❖ ❖

Lena: What do you call a rabbit that likes to swim with alligators?
Lulu: That's a mystery.
Lena: Dinner.

❖ ❖ ❖

Lena: What should you do if you can't find your snake?
Lulu: I'm blank.
Lena: Call the Missing Pythons Bureau.

Lena: What did the wicked chicken lay?
Lulu: It's unknown to me.
Lena: Deviled eggs.

❖   ❖   ❖

Lena: What did the arithmetic book say to the
psychiatrist?
Lulu: I'm in the dark.
Lena: I really have a lot of problems.

❖   ❖   ❖

Lena: What do you get if you cross a dentist and
a boat?
Lulu: Search me.
Lena: The tooth ferry.

❖   ❖   ❖

Lena: What do snakes do after a fight?
Lulu: I pass.
Lena: They hiss and make up.

37

Open the Door!

Knock, knock.
Who's there?
Buck and Ham.
Buck and Ham who?
Buck-and-Ham Palace.

❖ ❖ ❖

Knock, knock.
Who's there?
Hair Combs.
Hair Combs who?
Hair Combs the judge.

❖ ❖ ❖

Knock, knock.
Who's there?
Juan.
Juan who?
Juan two, buckle my shoe.

❖ ❖ ❖

Knock, knock.
Who's there?
Police.
Police who?
Police open the door.

❖ ❖ ❖

Knock, knock.
Who's there?
Sherwood.
Sherwood who?
Sherwood like to eat dinner with you.

❖ ❖ ❖

Knock, knock.
Who's there?
Radio.
Radio who?
Radio not, here I come.

❖ ❖ ❖

Knock, knock.
Who's there?
Cook.
Cook who?
Yes, you are crazy.

❖　❖　❖

Knock, knock.
Who's there?
Midas.
Midas who?
Midas well try again. . . . Knock, knock.

❖　❖　❖

Knock, knock.
Who's there?
Ferdie.
Ferdie who?
Ferdie last time, please open up.

❖　❖　❖

Knock, knock.
Who's there?
Marsha.
Marsha who?
Marsha Mallow.

38

Elton & Erwin

Elton: What did the chicken say when she laid a square egg?
Erwin: I have no clue.
Elton: Ouch!

❖ ❖ ❖

Elton: What kind of dancing do crash dummies enjoy?
Erwin: I don't know.
Elton: Break dancing.

❖ ❖ ❖

Elton: What lies at the bottom of the ocean and shivers?

Erwin: Beats me.
Elton: A nervous wreck.

❖ ❖ ❖

Elton: What is the saddest candy you can buy?
Erwin: I can't guess.
Elton: Glum drops.

❖ ❖ ❖

Elton: What is big, blows water from its spout,
and turns up once every 76 years?
Erwin: I have no idea.
Elton: Whaley's Comet.

❖ ❖ ❖

Elton: What did one sleepy pig say to the other
sleepy pig?
Erwin: You tell me.
Elton: Stop hogging the blankets!

❖ ❖ ❖

Elton: What is a frog's favorite sport?
Erwin: I give up.
Elton: Fly fishing.

❖ ❖ ❖

Elton: What do you call the period of time when nerds ruled the earth?
Erwin: Who knows?
Elton: The dork ages.

❖ ❖ ❖

Elton: What happened to the frog's car when the parking meter expired?
Erwin: You've got me.
Elton: It got toad away.

❖ ❖ ❖

Elton: What is the favorite play of pigs?
Erwin: My mind is blank.
Elton: Hamlet.

❖ ❖ ❖

Elton: What year do frogs like best?
Erwin: That's a mystery.
Elton: Leap year.

❖ ❖ ❖

Elton: What does a chicken say when he goes into a library?

Erwin: I'm blank.
Elton: Book-book-book-book-book-book!

❖ ❖ ❖

Elton: What do astronauts do when they're
 dirty?
Erwin: It's unknown to me.
Elton: They take a meteor shower.

❖ ❖ ❖

Elton: What is the favorite story of wild pigs?
Erwin: I'm in the dark.
Elton: Goldilocks and the Three Boars.

39

Camilla & Cora

Camilla: What kind of birds are most frequently kept in captivity?
Cora: I have no clue.
Camilla: Jail birds.

❖ ❖ ❖

Camilla: What is a liar's favorite month?
Cora: I don't know.
Camilla: Fib-ruary.

❖ ❖ ❖

Camilla: What happens when two frogs go after the same fly?

Cora: Beats me.
Camilla: They get tongue-tied.

❖ ❖ ❖

Camilla: What did Jonah say, when asked how he was feeling?
Cora: I can't guess.
Camilla: Very whale, thank you.

❖ ❖ ❖

Camilla: What do you get if you cross a hen with a banjo?
Cora: I have no idea.
Camilla: You get a self-plucking chicken.

❖ ❖ ❖

Camilla: What do chess players eat for breakfast?
Cora: You tell me.
Camilla: Pawncakes.

❖ ❖ ❖

Camilla: What TV news reporter sinks to the bottom of the ocean?
Cora: I give up.
Camilla: The anchorman.

❖ ❖ ❖

Camilla: What kind of storm moves the fastest?
Cora: Who knows?
Camilla: A hurry-cane.

❖ ❖ ❖

Camilla: What bird belongs in an insane asylum?
Cora: You've got me.
Camilla: A loon-atic.

❖ ❖ ❖

Camilla: What kind of vehicles do hitchhikers
  prefer?
Cora: My mind is blank.
Camilla: Pickup trucks.

❖ ❖ ❖

Camilla: What insect is hardest to understand
  when speaking?
Cora: That's a mystery.
Camilla: A mumble bee.

❖ ❖ ❖

Camilla: What animal hangs around caves and
  wins spelling bees?

Cora: I'm blank.
Camilla: An alpha-bat.

❖ ❖ ❖

Camilla: What happens to words when they break the law?
Cora: It's unknown to me.
Camilla: They get sentenced.

❖ ❖ ❖

Camilla: What game do little nerds like to play?
Cora: I'm in the dark.
Camilla: Hide-and-eek.

❖ ❖ ❖

Camilla: What locomotive wears sneakers?
Cora: Search me.
Camilla: A shoe-shoe train.

❖ ❖ ❖

Camilla: What ape helped settle the American frontier?
Cora: I pass.
Camilla: Daniel Ba-Boone.

40

Hobart & Herman

Hobart: What do you call a pig's underwear hanging on the clothesline?
Herman: I have no clue.
Hobart: Hogwash.

❖ ❖ ❖

Hobart: What does a dyslexic, atheist, insomniac do?
Herman: I don't know.
Hobart: He stays up all night wondering if there is a dog.

❖ ❖ ❖

Hobart: What ancient Egyptian beauty queen
  wore spiked running shoes?
Herman: Beats me.
Hobart: Cleats-o-patra.

❖ ❖ ❖

Hobart: What would you get if you crossed a
  flock of sheep and an Ice Age Elephant?
Herman: I can't guess.
Hobart: A very woolly mammoth.

❖ ❖ ❖

Hobart: What would you get if you crossed a
  rabbit with a mad doctor?
Herman: I have no idea.
Hobart: Hare-brained experiments.

❖ ❖ ❖

Hobart: What would you get if you crossed a
  magician with an alarm clock?
Herman: You tell me.
Hobart: A magic tick.

❖ ❖ ❖

Hobart: What do you always find at the end of
  a tunnel?

Herman: I give up.
Hobart: The letter "l."

❖ ❖ ❖

Hobart: What do horses do for entertainment?
Herman: Who knows?
Hobart: They watch stable TV.

❖ ❖ ❖

Hobart: What kind of doll do little girl bears
play with?
Herman: You've got me.
Hobart: Bearbie dolls.

❖ ❖ ❖

Hobart: What did the barber call his son?
Herman: My mind is blank.
Hobart: A little shaver.

❖ ❖ ❖

Hobart: What kind of bugs hang around bowl-
ing alleys?
Herman: That's a mystery.
Hobart: Bowl weevils.

❖ ❖ ❖

Hobart: What kind of trousers does a wise guy wear?
Herman: I'm blank.
Hobart: Smarty pants.

❖ ❖ ❖

Hobart: What do you know about the speed of light?
Herman: I don't have the foggiest.
Hobart: Only that it gets here too early in the morning.

❖ ❖ ❖

Hobart: What did Olaf say to his brother after his mother fell off the cliff?
Herman: It's unknown to me.
Hobart: Look Hans, no ma.

❖ ❖ ❖

Hobart: What happens when a room is full of jokesters?
Herman: I'm in the dark.
Hobart: Pun-demonium.

41

Mabel & Mavis

Mabel: What fruit is always complaining?
Mavis: I have no clue.
Mable: A crab apple.

❖　❖　❖

Mable: What did Aladdin name the flat-backed camel?
Mavis: I don't know.
Mable: Humphrey.

❖　❖　❖

Mable: What did Dumbo become when he didn't take a bath for a year?

Mavis: Beats me.
Mable: A smell-ephant.

❖　❖　❖

Mable: What river do pigs sail down in South
America?
Mavis: I can't guess.
Mable: The Hamazon river.

❖　❖　❖

Mable: What did one crow telephone operator
say to the other?
Mavis: I have no idea.
Mable: I have a caw for you.

❖　❖　❖

Mable: What kind of vegetable should we have
tonight?
Mavis: You tell me.
Mable: Beets me.

❖　❖　❖

Mable: What caramel-colored popcorn do ducks
like?
Mavis: I give up.
Mable: Quacker Jacks.

❖ ❖ ❖

Mable: What do you call talking birds who
adopt an orphan?
Mavis: Who knows?
Mable: Foster parrots.

❖ ❖ ❖

Mable: What is brown, lumpy, and wears a
coonskin cap?
Mavis: You've got me.
Mable: Gravy Crockett.

❖ ❖ ❖

Mable: What do you get when you burn the
candle at both ends?
Mavis: My mind is blank.
Mable: Smoke.

❖ ❖ ❖

Mable: What did they call Sleeping Beauty
after she skidded on a banana peel?
Mavis: That's a mystery.
Mable: Slipping Beauty.

❖ ❖ ❖

Mable: What type of songs does a lily sing to its children?
Mavis: I'm blank.
Mable: Lily-byes.

❖ ❖ ❖

Mable: What has many legs, antennae, and a sack of toys over its shoulder?
Mavis: It's unknown to me.
Mable: A Santa-pede.

❖ ❖ ❖

Mable: What happened when the hen went crazy?
Mavis: I'm in the dark.
Mable: It laid cracked eggs.

❖ ❖ ❖

Mable: What does a dog sleep in when camping?
Mavis: Search me.
Mable: A pup tent.

❖ ❖ ❖

Mable: What do you call a boar who has more than one wife?
Mavis: I pass.
Mable: A pigamist.

42

Roscoe & Rupert

Roscoe: What is an autobiography?
Rupert: I have no clue.
Roscoe: A car's life story.

❖ ❖ ❖

Roscoe: What is the first thing a little snake
learns in school?
Rupert: I don't know.
Roscoe: Hiss-tory.

❖ ❖ ❖

Roscoe: What does a shoehorn play?
Rupert: Beats me.
Roscoe: Footnotes.

❖ ❖ ❖

Roscoe: What did the parrot say to the street-
car?
Rupert: I can't guess.
Roscoe: Trolley want a cracker?

❖ ❖ ❖

Roscoe: What is the favorite musical instru-
ment of a shoe salesman?
Rupert: I have no idea.
Roscoe: A shoehorn.

❖ ❖ ❖

Roscoe: What do you call a TV series about
morons?
Rupert: You tell me.
Roscoe: A dope opera.

❖ ❖ ❖

Roscoe: What do jigsaw puzzles do when they
get bad news?
Rupert: I give up.
Roscoe: Go to pieces.

Roscoe: What do you say when choosing a cow?
Rupert: Who knows?
Roscoe: Eenie, meenie, miney, moo . . .

❖ ❖ ❖

Roscoe: What did the doctor order when the bull broke its leg?
Rupert: You've got me.
Roscoe: An ox-ray.

❖ ❖ ❖

Roscoe: What do you call thieves who steal windshield wipers?
Rupert: My mind is blank.
Roscoe: Windshield swipers.

❖ ❖ ❖

Roscoe: What do you say when choosing a hot dog?
Rupert: That's a mystery.
Roscoe: Weenie, meenie, miney, moe . . .

❖ ❖ ❖

Roscoe: What's Santa's ethnic background?
Rupert: I'm blank.
Roscoe: North Polish.

❖　❖　❖

Roscoe: What famous cowboy never said a
  word?
Rupert: I don't have the foggiest.
Roscoe: Quiet Earp.

❖　❖　❖

Roscoe: What is the slime's motto?
Rupert: It's unknown to me.
Roscoe: Goo for it.

❖　❖　❖

Roscoe: What is a cannibal's favorite game?
Rupert: I'm in the dark.
Roscoe: Swallow the Leader.

43

Knocked Out!

Knock, knock.
Who's there?
Annie.
Annie who?
Annie-body home?

❖ ❖ ❖

Knock, knock.
Who's there?
Cook.
Cook who?
Hey! Who are you calling cuckoo!

❖ ❖ ❖

Knock, knock.
Who's there?
Toodle.
Toodle who?
Toodle who to you too!

Knock, knock.
Who's there?
Barbie
Barbie who?
Barbie Q. Chicken.

Knock, knock.
Who's there?
Heaven.
Heaven who?
Heaven you heard this joke before?

❖ ❖ ❖

Knock, knock.
Who's there?
Amanda.
Amanda who?
Amanda to fix your TV.

❖ ❖ ❖

Knock, knock.
Who's there?
Cher.
Cher who?
Cher would be nice if you would open the door.

❖ ❖ ❖

Knock, knock.
Who's there?
Pasteur.
Pasteur who?
It's Pasteur bedtime.

❖ ❖ ❖

Knock, knock.
Who's there?
Carmen.
Carmen who?
"Carmen to my parlor," said the spider to the fly.

44

Trudy & Tobiah

Trudy: What do you get when a duck gives you
smart answers?
Tobiah: I have no clue.
Trudy: Wise quacks.

❖ ❖ ❖

Trudy: What is crisp, salty, and floats?
Tobiah: I don't know.
Trudy: Potato ships.

❖ ❖ ❖

Trudy: What do sharks eat at barbecues?
Tobiah: Beats me.
Trudy: Clamburgers.

❖ ❖ ❖

Trudy: What does Smokey the Bear spread on his toast?
Tobiah: I can't guess.
Trudy: Forest preserves.

❖ ❖ ❖

Trudy: What would you get if you mixed your mother's red nail polish with her orange nail polish?
Tobiah: I have no idea.
Trudy: In trouble.

❖ ❖ ❖

Trudy: What do mountaineers do when they're bored?
Tobiah: You tell me.
Trudy: They climb the walls.

❖ ❖ ❖

Trudy: What kind of music won't balloons dance to.
Tobiah: I give up.
Trudy: Pop music.

❖ ❖ ❖

Trudy: What did Tinkerbell play with as a young fairy?
Tobiah: Who knows?
Trudy: Tinker toys.

❖ ❖ ❖

Trudy: What is the difference between a generous host and a nasty snob?
Tobiah: You've got me.
Trudy: One puts people up and the other puts people down.

❖ ❖ ❖

Trudy: What kind of music do welders dance to?
Tobiah: My mind is blank.
Trudy: Heavy metal.

❖ ❖ ❖

Trudy: What is the first step in saving a person who is drowing?
Tobiah: That's a mystery.
Trudy: Take him out of the water.

❖ ❖ ❖

Trudy: Where does Mother Goose leave her garbage?
Tobiah: I'm blank.
Trudy: At the Humpty Dump.

❖   ❖   ❖

Trudy: Where do you send old detectives?
Tobiah: I don't have the foggiest.
Trudy: To the clue factory.

❖   ❖   ❖

Trudy: Where do crazy plants grow?
Tobiah: It's unknown to me.
Trudy: In cracked pots.

Other Books by Bob Phillips

For more information on how to
purchase other books and tapes by
Steve Russo; as well as information on
the *Real Answers* radio program, school
assemblies and crusades contact:

Real Answers with Steve Russo
P.O. Box 1549
Ontario, California 91762
909/466-7060
Fax: 909/466-7056